WHAT HAPPENS WHEN
School Starts Again

written + illustrated by
SARA OLSHER

mighty
+
bright

Hi, my name is Mia!

And this is Stuart. Stuart feels better when he knows what's going to happen every day.

(Actually, **everybody** feels better when they know what's going to happen - even grown-ups!)

Most of the time we do the same things in the mornings. We wake up.

We eat breakfast.
(I like apples.
Stuart only eats bugs.)

Usually nights are the same too.
We brush our teeth.

We put on jammies, and we go to bed. Every day ends with sleep.

But our days can be different.

MONDAY

TUESDAY

WEDNESDAY

THU

Some days we go to school, and some days are the weekend!

When something big changes, what we do each day can change too.
Stuart is getting used to some of the changes from the coronavirus.

But what he really wants to know is . . . **what about school?**

Because we're trying to keep people from getting sick,
more people are staying home in their houses, and
school might be different for awhile.

The truth is, grown-ups are still
figuring out what school will be like this year.

Some kids will start school at home, learning from a computer.
They will see their friends and teacher on the computer.

Teachers spent their summer vacation working hard to make learning
from home better, so you can learn new and exciting things.
They love you and want you to love school!

Your teacher will probably teach class right on the computer,
like Facetime or Zoom, and will be able to answer all your questions.

Sometimes there will be recorded videos from your teacher, and
your class will work together just like they do in the classroom —
which means you'll get to know all the kids in your class.

Other kids will learn on a computer for part of the time,
and go to school for part of the time.

If you **do** go to school, your class might have less kids
than it used to, and your desks will be further apart than
they used to be. You will probably have to wear a mask.

You'll also probably spend more time in your classroom than before. Instead of
eating lunch with the whole school, you might eat lunch with your class.

Your teacher will talk a **lot** about washing your hands.

For recess, the playground might not be open to play.
If that happens, there will be lots of other games to play!

Because grown-ups are still deciding about school,
all of **this might change** partway through the school year.

No matter what happens, kids will need to try their best to do their
work, help around the house and ask good questions.

You also might be wondering . . .
what about your favorite things to do **after** school?

Aftercare might be different — you might go different days, or not at all.

And afterschool activities might be different, too.
You might be able to play sports, but
you may need to wear a mask and
get your temperature taken.

And just like school, the decisions grown-ups
make about afterschool activities **might change.**

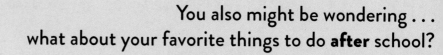

Not knowing exactly what's going to happen can be hard!

The good news is, grown-ups **do** know the important stuff:

1. They love you and will make good, safe choices
— so you don't need to worry.

2. They will help make a
plan so you know
what to expect.

Having a plan for each day will make everyone feel better.
You and your family can set up a plan just for you.

They'll help you understand when you'll be learning at home, and when you'll
be at school. And they'll help you plan fun activities, too!

Not seeing our friends every day can be hard, but we can help make it easier
by making sure we see their faces through Zoom, video chats or Facetime.

We can't have play dates, but video chats are fun too!

You can also make plans to move your body every day. Have a dance party! Do an exercise video online! Ride your bike in the driveway! Play soccer in the backyard with a family member!

FRIDAY

quiet time

9am-12pm

cook a meal

SATURDAY

Gramma + Grampa Smith

spa day

make a gift

SUNDAY

Lily

Even though there are some things we can't do right now, there are lots of things we **CAN** do. Your family can make plans to do things together that you might not usually have time for, including games, crafts, and reading together.

music

create kindness rocks™

LOVE

spa day

ead*

make a gift

puzzle or board game

cuddle time

take a walk

walk the dog

color or draw

There's also time to be creative by yourself. You can learn all sorts of things! Teach yourself to knit, sculpt with clay, make up songs, or help cook dinner.

This is also a good time to think of creative ways to show love to your neighborhood or city, especially because a lot of people feel lonely right now. Leave special messages on the ground with chalk, put drawings in your windows, or make paintings on rocks to leave outside for others to find.

Pretty much everyone wants things to go back to the way they were. Unfortunately, there's nothing you can do to make the coronavirus go away all by yourself. But you **can** do your part not to spread it.

Stuart doesn't quite remember what the coronavirus is, or how to make sure people don't get sick. Do you?

The coronavirus is a type of germ. When germs get inside our bodies, they can make us sick, and the coronavirus can make people **extra** sick.

Germs are suuuuper tiny, so you can't actually see them with your eyes.

Most germs don't make you sick. Our bodies are amazing and can kill them before they do. But if you've had a cold (which you probably have), you've had a virus.

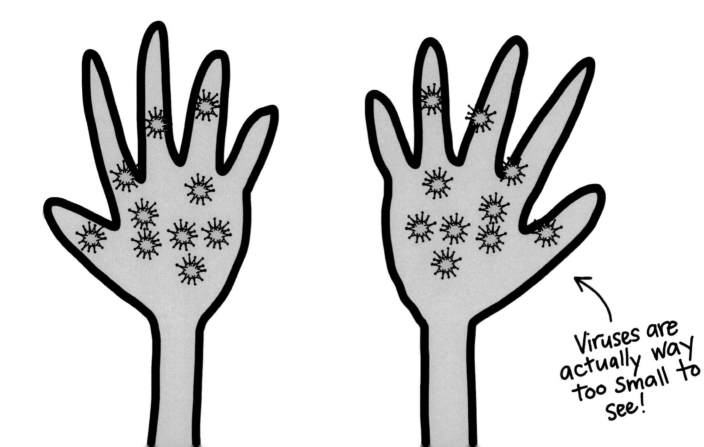

Viruses are actually way too small to see!

There are lots of things that people can do to keep from getting a virus. Most of these things you should do all the time even **without** the coronavirus.

don't sneeze into the air or into your hands. This is how your germs get in other people. Sneeze into your elbow.

wash your hands for 20 whole seconds! with soap!

don't pick your nose or touch your face or bite your nails— that's how germs get in!

The coronavirus is different than most viruses, because it can make people very sick, very easily. Because of that, we are doing even **more** to keep people from getting sick.

One way is by spending more time in our houses, and less time around other people.

When we are around other people, we are staying farther away from them than usual. We are pretending there's a **big, healthy bubble** around us, and the only people allowed in our bubbles are the people and pets who live in our house.

That way, people keep their virus to themselves!

And we also wear masks when we are inside
with people who don't live in our house.

This keeps our germs closer to our own bodies, so we don't get other
people sick, and we hopefully won't get sick ourselves.

Be a health hero! masks keep people from getting sick!

All of these changes can make you feel **mad** or **disappointed**, especially if you want to go to school or afterschool activities and aren't able to.

What's important is knowing that you can talk to your parents about your feelings, and remember — grown-ups are making these decisions because they **love you** and want to keep you and everyone else safe.

And the good news is, this won't last forever.

We will get back to our old plans — seeing our friends, going
outside, and doing what we always have — it just
might take awhile.

And even when Stuart
feels **mad** or **sad** or **scared**,
his family can help him
until the feeling goes away.

We can do hard things, together!

Make COVID-19 Easier on Kids
Show Your Kids What to Expect Each Day

Use a magnetic visual calendar, based on decades of science

Changes to your family's routines are hard on kids. They want to know what caused the change, but they also need to know how **their life** will be affected. Our calendars help kids understand what's happening, and when — which is proven to decrease their anxiety levels.

Learn more on our website:
http://mightyandbright.com/covid-19

Show online school, online math, and other school activities and responsibilities.

Encourage social interaction with Facetime/ video conferencing buttons for their friends and grandparents.

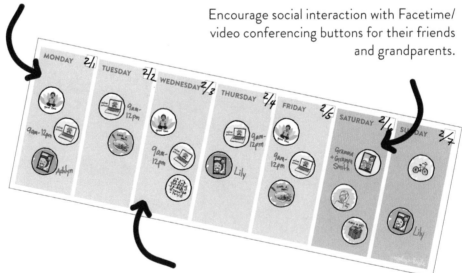

Add in activities — both active and creative — to add more structure to the day

Made in the USA
Middletown, DE
25 August 2020